Praise for *Church Locality*

If you believe churches should be intentional about *why* they exist and *how* they do ministry, then you should also believe *where* churches go is critically important. Jim and Tim have written an excellent resource on the importance of church locality. This book will help you understand how church location can extend the reach and impact of your congregation.

Thom S. Rainer
President, LifeWay Christian Resources

In an age of ministry specialization, Jim Tomberlin is a most helpful advocate for the church. Not only is Jim an expert of multisite components, he uniquely integrates the pieces together so that the local church as a whole is healthy and fruitful. I highly recommend this book. It is about church buildings for sure. But it's also about much more than that. It's about churches being on mission with Jesus.

Dave Bruskas, Teaching Pastor
Mars Hill Church
Seattle, WA

This book is must reading for all pastors, because all pastors must address locality (location plus facility) at some point in their ministries. You simply can't escape it. This was true of the Apostle Paul who was a strategic thinker and planner in the past to Pastor Paul who must be the same today. Gone are the days when we could take our facilities and setting for granted if ever there was such a time. As Bob Dillon warned, "The times they are a changing!" And the combination of the technological revolution, the multisite revolution and the economic recession attest to this. A great subtitle for this work is: *Everything You Want and Need to Know About Locality*. Wherever you are in terms of locality there's a chapter for you which demonstrates the value of this book.

Aubrey Malphurs
Founder of the Malphurs Group (TMG)
Professor of Leadership and Pastoral Ministries at Dallas Seminary

After helping churches launch in portable spaces for 20 years now, we have seen firsthand the challenges that Tomberlin and Cool bring up regarding where churches should meet. The "where" question is often overlooked so multi-sites and church planters will greatly benefit from this book.

Kevin Jones
Portable Church Industries.

Church Locality takes all the guess work out of finding the right church space for pastors and church planters. Jim Tomberlin and Tim Cool bring a ton of experience about a wide range of facility options. If you want to find the best space for your church to best serve your community, this is the book for you!

Dave Ferguson
Lead Pastor Community Christian Church
Author of *Exponential, On The Verge and Discover Your Mission Now*

The message of the Gospel remains unchanged but the world in which we seek to share it can be very different. While this can prove to be challenging, it can also yield discoveries of new opportunities to those who will ask the right questions and listen with an open mind. Jim Tomberlin & Tim Cool help us to ask the right questions and discover the right opportunities to better meet today's world with the Gospel Message.

Kevin Penry
Operations Leader, LifeChurch.tv
Oklahoma City, OK

This book is a great resource for anyone looking to go multisite and needs a practical framework to guide them to ensure all angles are thought through. Having worked with Tim on several projects, I know he understands the nuances of churches exploring multisite options.

Joshua Blackson
Operations & Expansion Pastor
Elevation Church, Charlotte, NC

The multisite movement has burst on the American scene in the past decade. Thousands of churches have now adopted the practices. There is a crying need for practical tools for church leaders to use to apply to facilities and finance decisions to help them continue their growth. *Church Locality* provides insight and tools for these decision makers to evaluate their future plans of gospel outreach.

Dave Travis
Managing Director
Leadership Network
Dallas, TX

What a great time to be in church ministry! Churches are learning and innovating like never before. Jim and Tim have written and compiled great wisdom from leading experts on the location and utilization of facilities for church purposes.

John Ortberg,
Senior Pastor
Menlo Park Presbyterian Church

Church is changing—things to consider regarding buildings, multisite, church planting and so many other matters. In navigating through these decisions, church leaders would benefit from the advice and counsel of those who have experience in these areas. Tim Cool and Jim Tomberlin are two such experts. I have known them both for a number of years and I have seen firsthand how churches benefit from the wisdom of their advice and counsel. Get the book, read it and let it guide your decision making. You won't regret it!

Jim Sheppard
CEO & Principal - Generis
Co-Author, Contagious Generosity

Church Locality is a practical book for where churches can and should meet. Because the material deals with the real-life issues of starting a new locality, I found myself digging in deep at so many points. When I was reading the sample letter to a City Mayor, I thought, "this is how a church should approach a city." If you are looking at starting a new locality for your church, this work will help you ask the right questions, consider the right issues and get the zoning permits!

Dr. David Fletcher
Founder, XPastor
Fullerton, CA

All the assumptions and rules concerning the use of sacred space have shifted. Church Locality is a helpful guidebook for church leaders to help them navigate the new rules for church buildings and utilization of existing facilities for ministry purposes.

Tony Morgan
Founder & Chief Strategic Officer
The Unstuck Group

Here's what I love about this book: It is current, it is quick, it is insightful, and it is resource-packed. Jim Tomberlin and Tim Cool have been part of the conversation that's helped us see the 'new rules' of church buildings are no longer fads and trends; they are realities. I'm for any book that helps reduce my headaches. Thanks, Jim and Tim, for doing just that.

Dr. Tom Nebel
Senior Strategist for the US Alliance for Church
Multiplication
Converge Worldwide

Jim and Tim are two highly respected experts and have written a great resource for multisite practitioners. Church Locality is filled with practical help. The truth is that finding the right building in the right place is critical to a successful launch. This book will help you determine where in your community and in what kind of facility your church can best reach people.

Dan Reiland
Executive Pastor, 12 Stone Church
Author of *Amplified Leadership*

As I read Church Locality, I kept saying to myself, 'Wow! They're right. I never thought of that before.' This is an excellent book that identifies—and addresses—obstacles to ministry effective-ness that most pastors don't even know they have.

Charles Arn, Ed.D.
President, Church Growth, Inc.

The rules have changed. Time was, to make room for more people, churches broke ground. No more. Today's fastest growing churches redesign programming, add services, launch multiple on-site worship venues, and then go multisite, more often than not using existing buildings. The multisite explosion has blasted away the greatest physical barriers to growth in our healthiest, fastest-growing churches. *Church Locality* is a wealth of how-to's—and a map of landmines to sidestep—for any church exploring multisite options. If you want to learn from the trial-and-error of the thousands of multi-site churches that have gone before rather than making the same mistakes all over again, you won't want to overlook this book.

Eddy Hall
Senior Consultant and CEO, Living Stones Associates
Coauthor, *When Not to Build and The More-with-Less Church*

Jim Tomberlin and Tim Cool have provided an excellent tool for churches to use as they consider church facilities today. Their unique perspective identifying how church facilities are utilized and maximized in the 21st century will guide your church as you sharpen your tool for your ministry.

John Muzyka
Service Realty Inc.
The Church Real Estate Professionals®

Tim has spent a lifetime developing deep understanding of the relationship between culture, ministry, leadership and facilities. He's also spent a lifetime developing a deep network of people who have drilled deeply with him. Many have collaborated with Tim here to compile vital information to equip you to be a great steward. In today's environment of limited resources, wisely stewarding our leadership and facility resources is not only Godly, but vital. The insight found here will help.

Ed Bahler
President, Aspen Group
Director, Future Travelers Group

Church Locality is like a field guide to help church leaders navigate a journey that can be filled with so many unknowns. It's hard enough for a church to know what to do with their existing campus, let alone considerations for multiple ones. Jim and Tim have written a practicality tool, equipping leaders to make informed ministry and facility decisions, in order to grow the Kingdom!

David Evans, AIA
President, Mantel Teter
Church Architectural Firm
Kansas City, MO

Jim Tomberlin is not only a pioneer in the multisite world. . .he stands at the cutting edge of what is possible and continues to push the boundaries. It is always a pleasure to work with a church after Jim has been involved, as they are always well prepared for the course they are on, understand the pitfalls and plateaus, and most importantly, they have a plan for success. Jim and Tim have provided a useful tool for church leaders who are expanding their borders.

Michael Gardner
Founder, Church On Wheels
Charlotte, NC

Church Locality is a must for growing churches. Jim, Tim, and their panel of experts draw on their vast experience to provide a structure for considering how best to utilize the space available to you. This is a great tool for any pastor's toolbox.

Justin Lathrop
Leadership Network Prime Solutions
Dallas, TX

Church Locality

New Rules for Church Buildings in a Multisite, Church Planting, and Giga-Church World

Jim Tomberlin and Tim Cool

Published by Rainer Publishing
www.rainerpublishing.com

ISBN 978-0692203132

Printed in the United States of America

Foreword

I remember the feeling in my stomach when our local government said "no" to our request to build a larger building for our rapidly growing congregation. What were we going to do? How will we possibly move forward?

We were doing five services in cramped facilities. Our staff was exhausted. The idea of starting yet another service in a less than desirable times slot was not appealing.

Fortunately we met a group of church leaders grappling with similar issues, one of whom was Jim Tomberlin. We agreed to meet together twice a year for the next two years to see if we could find some solutions to what more and more churches were facing: growing congregations and fewer opportunities to expand on existing properties.

Out of those gatherings came a loose framework for what has now been called "the multisite revolution". What started as a desperate search for immediate solutions has morphed into a growing movement that is changing how church is being done in our generation.

Jim Tomberlin has continued to serve the movement by gathering best practices and making them available to churches around the world who are expanding their ministries to more than one location.

In this latest book, *Church Locality: New Rules for Church Buildings in a Multisite, Church Planting, and Giga-Church World*, Jim and co-author Tim Cool unpack some practical tools to use when thinking about buildings and site selection for new campuses and church plants. They use research and common sense to help leaders maximize God given momentum and avoid costly mistakes in the selection of new ministry locations.

These are exciting days for the church. New technology and paradigm shifts concerning geographical boundaries have opened the doors to new ways to do church and reach people who may be far from God.

The playing field has changed and the rules are different. In the pages of this book you will find some guidelines that will help you navigate the new reality.

As you read it, never forget that God is "able to do immeasurably more than all we ask or imagine, according to his power that is at work within us" (Ephesians 3:20 NIV). Allow Him to open your mind to His limitless possibilities.

Greg Surratt
Pastor, Seacoast Church
President, The Association of Related Churches (ARC)

Contents

Introduction

I (Tim) was raised in the home of a pastor. I did not realize that my father was a church planter, but that's what he was. Of course, back then they were called "pioneer pastors." At least, that is what his denomination called them.

I can remember my parents starting the church in our living room. The students met in the basement. The children were taught in bedrooms. There in the Buffalo suburb of West Seneca, New York, a church of a few families was birthed. We met weekly in our home until the attendance was too much for our house.

So what is a church to do? A kitchen overflow room is not a good long-term solution. What does a growing church do when the pastor's house just is not enough? In our case we moved into a local fire station. They would back out the trucks, and we would move in metal folding chairs. Dad led worship with his accordion, so we had our own portable band wherever we went. This continued until we out grew that space, and the next stop was a local Christian college...then finally, to our own building.

If you have ever been part of a church plant or the launching of a multisite congregation, then the above story most likely sounds familiar (minus the accordion). One of the biggest differences from my life story in 1968 (yes, I am old) to now, is that most church plants have a much better road map to follow.

Most church leaders I know have either been part of a movement, large parent church, or church planting organization that has helped to get them started. The emergence of giga-size churches (over 10,000 in weekend attendance) and churches with multiple campuses has pushed us into a new era in North America.

Additionally, with church planting on an upward trajectory, we see a new wave of church growth for the next several decades. Megachurches are getting bigger because they are no longer limited to one location.

For example, LifeChurch.tv based in Oklahoma City is the largest church in America with over 50,000 in attendance across 18 campuses in several states. To give you some perspective on the rapid growth of the giga-church, church planting, and multisite movements, here are a few stats:

Megachurch Facts

- There are 1,650 megachurches in America, according to *Leadership Network*.
- 5 million people attend a megachurch every week in America.
- 10% of Protestant church-goers attend a megachurch.
- 46 US states and Washington DC have megachurches.
- 72 of the largest churches in America are giga-churches with an average of over 10,000 in weekend attendance.

Multisite Facts

- In 1990, there were 10 multisite churches.
- In 1998, that number had expanded to about 100.
- In late 2005, there were more than 1,500 multisite churches in the United States.
- In mid-2008, there were an estimated 2,000 multisite churches across the US.
- In 2014 there are now more than 8,000 multisite churches in North America, according to *Leadership Network*.

- Multisite churches are succeeding in urban, suburban, and rural communities, as well as internationally.
- The pace of multisite growth is increasing. This movement will continue.

Church Planting Facts

- In most regions of the United States, less that 20% of people attend a Christian church any given weekend.
- If we were to start new churches of 1,000 people each, then we would need over 200,000 new churches in the United States to reach those who do not attend church regularly.
- Over 80% of people who attend a church plant are unchurched and spiritually disenfranchised.
- The United States has the 4th largest population of unreached people in the world, after India, China, and Malaysia.
- The United States is 14th on the list of nations *receiving* missionaries from other countries.

It's not cliché; the fields are ripe. The need is evident. It is also clear that the means and methods of impacting our culture and communities of the past century are no longer effective for reaching the masses of people far from Christ.

The emergence of multisite strategies, the resurgence of church planting and the exponential growth of giga-churches are changing the church building conversation across the nation.

Growing churches today are utilizing multisite and church planting strategies to reproduce themselves for greater outreach and impact.

But where? That is the purpose of this book. This book is not intended to address the *why* of these missional approaches or even the *how*. This book is a tool and guide to the *where.*

Where should we meet? What kind of facilities are usable for churches? What are the implications of the various options? This book is all about the locations and facilities that reproducing churches are utilizing to extend their reach and impact.

Here is the formula that defines this work: *Location + Facility = Locality.*

Almost weekly, Jim and I are asked a whole host of questions surrounding the "where" question. These questions include:

1. How much space do we need?
2. Can we make a warehouse work for our ministry?
3. Is a school a better option than leasing retail space, or should we buy land and build?
4. How much will it cost to up-fit retail/commercial space?
5. Where should we plant a church?
6. Where should we launch a multisite campus?
7. How close should our campuses be to one another?

These questions are just the tip of the proverbial iceberg when a church is looking at leasing, renting, or borrowing a facility to function. There are so many questions that need to be asked and answered *before* you commit to a lease or purchase agreement. While the excitement for having a potential home for your church or campus is almost intoxicating, you need to step back and complete your due diligence.

To help you, we have developed this guide to make your process easier...well, maybe not easier, but definitely more informed.

CHAPTER ONE

The Changing Landscape of Church Space

In 1989 popular author Ken Follett wrote a riveting best-selling novel *Pillars of the Earth* about the factors impacting the building of cathedrals in the Middle Ages. Those factors influenced church construction and facility use for nearly a millennium. Today there are new factors that are dramatically shifting the way we build and utilize church facilities. We believe that the most relevant shifts in the use and development of ministry spaces can be summarized in six new pillars.

Pillar 1: The Technological Revolution

Technology affects church locality. When I (Jim) came to my church in Colorado in 1991 the latest technology was the overhead projector. Today we have personal computers, digital video, Wi-Fi, smartphones, cloud computing, social media, and Internet campuses. Typically the first impression people have of a church is a virtual one on

Facebook, a website, or online campus. People no longer need to place their feet on your specific church location to begin to form their opinions about your congregation.

During the Middle Ages, church leaders taught the illiterate masses biblical content through images made of colored stained glass in the church windows. Now we teach biblical content with images on video screens. Historically, the vast majority of people heard God's Word proclaimed in a church building. Then there was radio. Then TV. Then cassette tapes and CDs. Then podcasts. Today all we need is a smart phone to stream a message.

This technological revolution is making the ministry of a local church less facility-centric. While the primary ministry of a church is local, it doesn't have to be limited to a geographical location or tied to a facility. Cloud computing makes the universal church more... universal. Any local congregation can deliver a message anytime, anywhere on the planet.

New Rule: The technological revolution has extended church impact beyond the walls of a building and geographic location.

Pillar 2: The Multisite Church Revolution

Churches are no longer limited to one location. All of these technological breakthroughs have had a profound impact on how we build, develop, and utilize church facilities today. They also have laid the foundation for the multisite church revolution. In the last quarter of the twentieth century growing churches had only one option, expand through buying more land and building larger facilities. Many of these churches became megachurches of 2,000+ people in weekend attendance through a series of steps.

Many of these churches bought large tracts of land in suburban communities and built large worship centers with corresponding children and youth spaces. Their parking lots are bigger than the local mall. They added multiple worship services on multiple days (Saturdays and Sundays). Eventually many of these churches became landlocked or restricted by zoning laws that prevented further expansion on their campus.

To accommodate and accelerate growth they created closed-circuit television overflow rooms in fellowship halls, gymnasiums, chapels, and student centers on the existing church campus. With the advent of digital technology these "overflow" settings eventually evolved into high quality video venues. It was inevitable that these video venues on the existing campus would evolve into video venues off campus, giving birth to the multisite church revolution. Now churches have an alternative to buying land and building bigger buildings in one location. They can grow through multiple locations. They don't have to put all their resources into one location.

New Rule: The multisite revolution liberated churches from overbuilding unsustainable mega-campuses.

Pillar 3: The Economic Recession

Before the multisite revolution we often bought large tracts of land and built huge facilities because we could. Today the economic reality has changed the equation. Growing a church through multiple sites made reasonable sense in prosperous times, but during the economic recession of 2008-2010 it became the primary way growing churches were accommodating their growth and extending their reach.

New church construction dramatically dropped off during the recession while adding sites dramatically increased. Few multisite churches buy land and build new facilities. Instead they tend to rent or purchase existing facilities and retrofit them. Half of all multisite campuses start in a school, ten percent begin in theaters, and a third come through a church merger or acquisition. Eventually most multisite campuses rent or purchase a long-term 24/7 facility.

Even as the economy slowly recovers, there will be less appetite for purchasing enormous tracts of land and spending millions of dollars on one location when you can multisite for a fraction of the cost. The average cost of launching a multisite campus in a school or theater is between $250,000 and $500,000. The cost of retrofitting an existing commercial building costs between $750,000 and $1.5 million, depending on the size, scope, and location of the project. While adding sites is not cheap, it is much less expensive than buying more land or building larger buildings. This financial reason is why the majority of megachurches have multiple campuses. Adding sites allows churches to reach more people better, faster, and cheaper than by building a massive church campus in one location.

New Rule: The economic recession liberated churches from excessively expensive building campaigns.

Pillar 4: The Decline in Church Attendance

There are many pundits today who suggest the church in America is dying, but to paraphrase Mark Twain, the reports of the church's death have been greatly exaggerated. In the 1950s, a greater proportion of Americans went to church, or at least, they *said* they went to church because the culture valued it more.

Though there are many biblically-centered, vibrant, and growing churches in America today, there has been a clear shift away from the value of church attendance. Biblical Christianity is growing in America; cultural Christianity is in decline. Most Americans declare themselves spiritual but not religious. Today less than 20% of Americans attend church regularly.

The church building was once seen as a key asset in the community. Today, these same buildings can be viewed as a liability. In the eyes of people who do not value church attendance, church buildings reduce potential tax revenue, cause traffic headaches, and create noise pollution.

As a result there is an increasing community resistance to churches buying land and building facilities, especially large facilities. To win the hearts of the secular community church buildings will have to be multi-purpose facilities that not only serve the church family but also the broader local community.

New Rule: The decline in church attendance is forcing churches to build community-centric, multi-purpose, and environmentally-friendly facilities.

Pillar 5: The Church Planting Resurgence

The church heroes of the Boomer generation were the megachurch pastors. Today they are the church planters. When I started thinking about multisite churches in the early-1990s, I thought it would be like church-planting. So I went and bought all the church-planting books available (all three of them).

Not only were there not many books about church planting, the few that were available were either written by researchers who had never started a church themselves or by individuals who were successful church planters in the 1950s.

Today there are about three books a month published about church planting from successful practitioners. Starting new churches is popular, and that's a good thing!

In the past local churches gave money to their denominations or networks, and their denomination or network started churches. Today local churches still give money to their denominations and networks, but increasingly local churches are planting churches as well.

Local pastors and churches are passionately embracing the responsibility of starting new congregations. A few of them are creating networks of reproducing churches through multiple sites and church planting. Some of them are becoming movements that are driven by a local church instead of a national denominational headquarters.

These new church planters are less inclined towards building mega campuses. Rather, they tend to repurpose existing buildings in the community.

When they do build facilities, they will be smaller (under 1,500 seats) and multi-purpose with multiple venues that are community and environmentally friendly.

New Rule: The church planting resurgence is retro-fitting existing commercial facilities and will build smaller church facilities with multiple venues.

Pillar 6: The Church Merger Trend

Roughly 80 percent of the 320,000 Protestant churches in the United States have plateaued or are declining. Many of these churches have empty facilities in desperate need of a vibrant ministry. Among the 20 percent of growing, vibrant congregations across the United States, many are in desperate need of space. This reality is generating a new kind of mission-driven merger that is recycling old church buildings. Already one out of three multisite campuses is the result of a church merger. I co-authored *Better Together: Making Church Mergers Work* with Warren Bird to help churches maximize this option.

In addition, there is a pastor succession tidal wave coming because so many Protestant pastors are approaching retirement. The next ten years will see an annual mass exodus of senior pastors retiring or leaving their position to pursue other ministry options. Who will fill these pulpits? The multisite model will play an increasing role in this process. I predict that we will see more senior pastors coming from campus pastors and through church mergers in the next decade.

The merger and succession trends present an opportunity to recycle and redeem a huge inventory of existing church buildings to meet the expectations of church goers today. The church buildings of the twenty-first century will require more high-tech and intimate worship settings, high quantity and quality community gathering spaces, and cutting-edge children's environments that are open, colorful, and secure.

New Rule: The church merger trend is redeeming and recycling existing church buildings for renewed use.

Church leaders, church architects, and church building companies who can embrace these shifts will survive and thrive.

Those who cannot will go the way of the dinosaur.

CHAPTER TWO

What's the Future of the Church Building?

by Ed Stetzer

The megachurch has been a topic of interest for years. There are more every year and their growth rate is increasing. In other words, it's not just that there are more, their rate of increase is growing.

Yet, when most people think of megachurches they not only think of mega-numbers, but also mega-facilities. Some megachurches have begun to think differently about their facilities.

The last church I pastored had a 3,000 seat sanctuary. That's a big room. But, what is interesting is that the church would not build that building if they could do it again, and that's a theme I consistently hear. So what are the trends in big church buildings today?

One of the trends I have observed in a qualitative way is that fewer churches are building large spaces specifically meant to accommodate thousands of people. In 2009 I did research on gathering spaces of 5,000 seats or more. It would seem that being a megachurch does not necessarily imply having mega-facilities even if they maintain mega-numbers. While the number of megachurches has increased, sanctuaries have not grown at the same pace.

While the number of megachurches has increased, my (unscientific) observation is that sanctuaries have not grown at the same pace. At the time I did the research, the average main sanctuary seating capacity in the typical American megachurch was 1,400 at most. This is large, but nowhere near 5,000. It seems that gathering spaces of growing megachurches continue to get smaller.

There seems to have been a substantial shift from the days of several thousand-seat sanctuaries to smaller venues. There are certainly exceptions, but I'm sensing a trend.

The decline of large church buildings points to a shift in ministry methodology. Many of the largest churches have begun to favor multisite expansion or church planting partnerships. While the large, larger, and largest churches continue to grow ever larger, they do not require larger spaces in the process—just more spaces (which tend to still be large!).

Simply put, implementing the multisite model compresses down the magnitude of the cavernous sanctuary. And, I do wonder if such buildings might be combined with a better multiplication strategy for a greater community impact.

The largest megachurches often grow by adding sites and services rather than square footage to their buildings. At least in the American context today, the giga-church, consisting of 10,000 or more members or attendees, often grows by adding sites and services rather than square footage to their buildings. New Spring Church in South Carolina provides a prime example. Pastored by Perry Noble, New Spring runs about 23,000 people on a given Sunday. However, their campuses do not seat 10,000 or even 5,000. Instead, there are multiple services and multiple technological means to distribute the message to other campuses.

Similar models like Saddleback implement video technology on many different sites, which allows those models to have 20,000 or more people attending their church on a weekly basis. Ultimately, the growth has shifted drastically away from continual building expansion to continual site expansion. As Rick Warren explained to me recently, their growth happens like a tree—not at the trunk, but at the branches. My guess is we will hear more thinking like that in years to come—smaller (but still very big) buildings, with more locations that are also smaller.

This trend is not only true of giga-churches, but seems to the trajectory of megachurches also. One example is Calvary Baptist Church in Winston-Salem, NC. Calvary is an older established church that has little room to expand at their central campus. Under the leadership of their former pastor Al Gilbert, Calvary voted to open a second campus in an area of town where over 30% of their existing members already lived.

The attendance at Calvary's new campus has more than doubled over the last 3 years, many of the new members having no prior connection to Calvary. That would have been unheard of a few decades ago.

So what are the benefits of a multisite mega-ministry? Part of the point is not really "new" news: more and more megachurches are multiplying their ministry through multi-campus ministry. Perhaps you remember Warren Bird's recent research that demonstrated multisite churches reach more people than single site churches, multisite tends to spread healthy churches to more diverse communities, and multisite churches have more volunteers in service as a percentage than single site.

Additionally, multisite churches baptize more people than single site. Multisite churches tend to activate more people into ministry than single site. However, my additional point is that multisite may very well lead to smaller (and, I hope) recyclable buildings that do not lead to a proliferation of large, empty church caverns when neighborhoods change.

Megachurches have shifted their philosophy from building bigger and bigger to spreading further and further. Also, part of the megachurch debate centered on whether or not the model could sustain itself in years to come. Since then, megachurches have shifted their philosophy from building bigger and bigger to spreading further and further through multisite ministry. I imagine that will improve sustainability as well.

Will the megachurch movement endure? It is quite possible that the evangelical landscape will include more megachurches than ever in the future. Why? Well, churches grow. Then they grow more...and then they grow some more.

While the evangelical landscape will include more megachurches than ever, I would contend that the vast majority of those megachurches will be multisite churches. Whether you like the megachurch or not, the trends point to the fact that the megachurch phenomenon is not over, but it is actually increasing in its growth.

Furthermore, I think it is now beginning to get its second wind through the multisite expansion model. When it comes to the megachurch the model of bigger church buildings is declining, but new campuses are springing to life all over the landscape.

It appears that bigger churches are having smaller buildings and more locations. There are lots of implications here—some good and some bad. But, it appears that bigger churches are having smaller buildings—and more locations. I'm not sure I know all the implications of this yet, but a new reality is emerging and—with all such shifts—it promises both challenges and opportunities.

CHAPTER THREE

All Ministry is Local (Mostly)

In Chicago where I (Jim) lived for five years, a politician's career can be determined by how quickly snow and garbage is removed from the streets. Politicians live and die by a simple mantra, "All politics is *local.*" At the end of the day what concerns most people isn't what is happening across the nation or around the world, but what is going on in their own backyard, neighborhood, or town. In a similar way, most church ministry like politics, is *local.*

One of the most amazing and consistent facts about church attendance is that the majority of church-goers live within a 15-minute drive of their church building. The rest live within 30 minutes. If you don't believe it, just ask the next time you are with a group of church goers how many live within 15 minutes of their church, then 30 minutes.

Only a very few, if any, will drive more than 30 minutes to church. Though most churches have national and international initiatives—the majority of their time, money, and energy is spent on people who live within 15 minutes driving time. Why? All ministry (or at least most of it) is *local.* This is not a bad thing. Local churches are meant to be *local.*

While every local church has a global mandate to fulfill the Great Commission, the going and sending is always to a specific locality. And local churches that grow through multisite strategies will have most campuses that are within 10 to 30 minutes of the birthing campus.

Those well-known multisite churches with campuses all over the country only represent 2% of all the multisite churches in North America. Multisite is all about putting the *local* back into the local church by taking church to the people!

All churches, even healthy ones, will plateau in attendance over time because of their stage in the church life cycle and/or ministry saturation. Instead of relocating and abandoning their current location, churches can multiply themselves into the next community while continuing to serve their current one. This is one of the most compelling reasons for churches to consider a multisite strategy.

When a church begins to think about going multisite I recommend map-pointing their church database to determine where their church attenders are coming *from*. Anyone who has completed a guest card, dropped a child off in the children's program, joined or contributed to your church should be in your church database and are candidates to help launch a multisite campus in their community.

Once you have pinpointed the households that attend your church on a map, draw a ring around the 15-minute driving-time around your church. Launch your multisite campuses wherever there are large pockets of households near the 15-minute perimeter of your church.

I call it the Henry Blackaby method of launching campuses. In his bestselling book *Experiencing God*, Blackaby describes how to experience God by asking God to show you where He is working. When God shows you where He is working that becomes the invitation to join Him in His work. When it comes to multisite locations, find out where God is bringing people to your church around the 15-minute driving perimeter.

Once He shows you that's the invitation to join Him there by taking your church to that community. This is the primary reason multisite campuses have such a high success rate. They are not going to a new community; they are already there with a significant base of equipped people with their church DNA.

The church in the New Testament is often described geographically—the Church of Jerusalem, Corinth, Ephesus, Colossae, Antioch, or Rome. Why? All ministry is *local* (mostly).

Go take your church to the people!

CHAPTER FOUR

What Church Buildings Cannot Do

Church locality is important. Church facilities are public places for corporate worship and ministry that establish presence in a local community. A facility creates a sense of stability and permanence. However, facilities are not a panacea. We have heard countless times the failed "Field of Dreams" philosophy. You know it...*Build it and they will come*...or maybe...*Rent it and they will come*. It worked for Kevin Costner in a corn field— not so much for churches.

We are *not* suggesting that facilities don't help you fulfill your vision and mission. They do. However, we *are* saying that using a facility as your magic pixy dust to church growth is severely flawed. You're dreaming if you think a building can produce long-term numerical and spiritual growth in a congregation.

So, what are some of the things a church building cannot do? Buildings do not preach sermons. Buildings do not create relationships. Buildings do not reach people. Buildings do not save people. These items are obvious. Here are three common misconceptions about church buildings:

1. **A building stimulates growth.** If your church is not already growing, a new building is not likely going to jump-start growth. People think, "If we build it, then they will come." If we build it, then the building is going to create excitement. But if your growth is not the primary factor for increasing your physical space, then building or relocating will not stimulate your growth. We have actually seen instances where the opposite has happened and the expansion initiative has put the church in decline, because the rationale was wrong.

2. **A building improves members' giving to ministry.** Again, if the congregation is not already giving and living a life of generosity, then a facility project will not get them to become regular contributors. You might do a campaign and you might have some people start giving to the project, but that is different than developing a congregation of generous givers as a lifestyle.

3. **A building motivates people to minister.** A building project will not compel people outward. If you build a building or lease a shopping center prior to establishing a culture of evangelism, outreach and service, then all your people will move inward. Apart from an existing culture of outreach, new buildings push people into a holy huddle. A new building can promote a sense of "arrival" and a tendency to cocoon in the new digs. I (Tim) was part of a fast growing church back in the 1990s that had an incredible culture of service, ministry, and outreach…then…we built a lovely new sanctuary with pews and a permanent sound system…meaning no weekly setup required in the gym, to name just one change the new building caused. The culture of the church became one of a country club (with "member privileges") instead of a community of missionaries to their culture.

Here's a facility quiz. This test will help you identify your rationale for a facility. Answer TRUE or FALSE to each of the following statements:

1. A building will attract new people to the church.

2. Members will be more motivated to reach out to others once we have a building.
3. A building will inspire people to worship.
4. A building program will involve more people in the work of the church.
5. A facility initiative will motivate our people to give more generously to the work of the church.
6. A facility initiative will unify our people behind a significant challenge.
7. A building will make a statement to the community about our church's importance.
8. Our people will take greater pride in the church when a new building is ready to occupy.
9. A new facility will provide our people with a more effective tool for ministry.

If you answered TRUE to any of the first eight statements, you probably need to reevaluate your motive to build. Number nine is truly the only motivating factor that should be leading us to build a new facility: To create an effective tool for ministry. Your church building is not ministry; it's a tool for ministry. And your church locality helps determine the type of ministry you do.

I (Jim) have been in church buildings almost every week of my entire adult life. I served four churches in my three decades of being a pastor. I rented, constructed, and renovated church facilities in every one of the churches I served. For the past ten years I've consulted hundreds of churches that have rented, constructed, and renovated church facilities. I have partnered with church architects and church construction companies to help build, renovate, and recycle church facilities.

I love church buildings. I have thousands of church photos in my photo library to prove it. There are a few things buildings cannot do. For any congregation considering a change involving the church building—whether renovation, new building, or multisite—let's lower our expectations about the actual facility. And let's raise our expectations about how God can use the people in the building.

Buildings don't reach people, people reach people. As stated earlier, "build it and they will come" is a myth—so is launching a multisite campus and they will come. Inadvertently we have defined church success as a building, and the bigger the building, the greater the success. In reality, success is about taking ministry to the people by *being* the church in a community, not by building a church facility.

Buildings don't change people, Jesus does. The first three centuries of the Christian faith changed the world without constructing or owning a building. They met in existing facilities and homes.

God does not live in church buildings. God dwells in human beings. The Apostle Paul made it very clear on Mars Hill in Athens "God doesn't live in man-made temples" (Acts 17:24). He explained it further to the believers in Corinth, "Don't you realize that all of you together are the temple of God and that the Spirit of God lives in you?" (1 Corinthians 3:16). The Apostle Peter concludes, "And now God is building you, as living stones, into his spiritual temple" (1 Peter 2:5).

Buildings are a means to the end, not the end game. Buildings are tools. Church buildings are public places for corporate worship that establish presence and commitment to a local community.

Local churches are local. The majority of church attenders live within 15 minutes driving time of their church building, the rest live within 30 minutes. The majority of a church's time, energy and resources are spent locally. Church success is not defined by a building, but by transformed lives and communities.

If the above are misconceptions about church buildings, what trends are we seeing?

- One church in multiple locations in suburban, rural and urban settings.
- Giga-size churches with over 10,000 weekend attendance on multiple smaller campuses.
- Fewer seats per location (under 1,500) and spread over multiple venues at that location.
- Multisite campuses and church planting through existing facilities (schools, theaters, commercial space, churches).
- Successful mission-driven church mergers (as opposed to the failed survival-driven mergers of the past).
- Multi-purpose, local community-centric and environmental-friendly buildings.
- The pew has left the building for more comfortable and individual theater-style seating.
- High-tech and intimate worship settings with large lobbies and wide halls.
- Moving the youth services to an evening gathering and utilizing the youth center as a video venue service on Sunday mornings.

- Multiple high quality community gathering spaces, such as Wi-Fi cafes and conference rooms.
- Cutting-edge children's environments that are open, colorful, and secure.
- The decline in building church parlors, fellowship halls, and gymnasiums.

What are the facility options for churches that are plateaued, declining or growing?

- Revitalize through a ministry turnaround.
- Renew through a strategic partnership.
- Rebirth through a church merger.
- Recycle and renovate current facilities.
- Release through legacy (selling church property and giving the money to other kingdom endeavors).
- Reproduce by facility expansion, multisiting or planting new congregations.
- Rent and retrofit commercial facilities.

What's in your church building future?

CHAPTER FIVE

Redemptive Engineering

If you have ever been involved in a church development project, you have probably heard the term "value engineering." For many of you, that sends chills down your spine and causes you to have cold sweats. Perhaps some of you debating even reading this chapter because of the word "engineering."

Generally speaking, value engineering means you reduce the scope of a project in order to cut costs to fit within a budget, either because the project was over-designed or the financial condition of the church has changed. Fortunately, redemptive engineering is not value engineering.

I first heard this term used by my friend Armando Fullwood with WAVE, a global audio visual designer and integrator. He has used this term to describe their philosophy of looking for ways to "repurpose" existing items when they are working on a new design for a church. They look for opportunities to reduce the total project budget by finding ways to reuse speakers, microphones, or mixers, etc., either within the new design or within the campus in some other desired function.

Over the past several years I (Tim) have seen other examples of redemptive engineering that goes beyond audio and visual systems and encompasses many other aspects of church development projects. Let me give you some examples with the hope that they will spur creative thinking for you and your church.

Redemptive Engineering: Reallocation of Space

I cannot tell you how many times I hear churches say "we need to build new space" or "we do not have enough space." In many of these cases, the issue is not "space" but the use and allocation of the space they already have. For those of you who are Southern Baptist, do you remember what the "Sunday School Board" used to recommend for educational space?

It was a large meeting room with all of the small classrooms around the perimeter. Many of these perimeter rooms were smaller than a janitor's closet. But what may look like a janitor's closet today can be redeemed for better space. These spaces have been relegated to storage areas so we think we do not have enough space, when in reality, we may have more space than we realize. I would rather see a church spend $50-75/SF to renovate a facility than to spend $145/SF for new construction. Are we not better to *redeem* the space we already have than to build more space that we have to heat/cool and maintain?

Redemptive Engineering: Redesign of Space

At First Christian Church, Huntington Beach, CA the church had an older, "tired" campus that needed a major face list. They had a sanctuary with a 1970 motif, complete with the typical steep sloped "A" frame roof. Instead of demolishing the building, the design professionals worked with the church to see how it could fit in the "story" the church wanted to tell to the community.

As a result, the building was transformed into a wonderful chapel that fit the campus and helped tell the story. While not every church may have the potential for this drastic transformation, you should consider the possibilities of your current campus before planning to demolish or move. Transforming an existing out-of-date building makes a statement and gets your community talking. And it may just be less expensive.

Redemptive Engineering: Redeem the Space

Redemptive engineering can help involve more people in the creative process of transformation. In one example, a church utilized the people of the congregation to transform their children's space. In thinking through the space and the story of the church, it was suggested that a non-traditional tree-house venue would best suit the children's ministry. When building a tree house what do most people use?

I know we built ours out of scrap material we could find in the garage and backyard. So why should this new children's venue be any different? In the end, it was suggested that the parents provide old milk crates to use as seats in the kids worship area. Not only did they redeem unused materials (and keep them out of the city landfill), they also created a story about the space and saved money doing it. Another positive benefit of this project was the church family got to be involved and participate in the transformation of the space.

Redemptive Engineering: Renovate the Space

For the first time in my adult life, I have owned a vehicle long enough to have the state issue a new license plate instead of just sending new stickers. As I took the old plate off I was reminded of a project I visited in Spring, TX. This church wanted to develop a facility that would provide a rustic appearance. Until a few years ago, Texas would issue a new licenses plate every year in lieu of a sticker.

If you lived in Texas for any period of time, just think how many old plates you might have in your garage. So as part of the design, they incorporated the use of old license plates as exterior cladding on a portion of the facade. Not only did the plates give the facility a fresh look, they redeemed materials that would have otherwise ended up in a junk yard.

So, as you plan a new facility, do not get sucked in to the myth of "all things new." Look around and see what you can redeem. As the church, we are in the business of redeemed lives. So why not redeem other items God has entrusted us with?

CHAPTER SIX

The Big Box Church Building

For the past few years we have seen lots of churches take advantage of the vacancy rates in many of the country's lagging real estate markets. The exit of Circuit City, Linens 'n Things, and Block Buster, the relocation of Wal-Mart to make way for the super store, the downsizing of many car dealerships, and the closing of other large retail facilities has left the real estate landscape cluttered with an abundance of empty "big box" spaces. More than a few churches have seized the opportunity to occupy these buildings.

These big box church locations can be advantageous for the right church in the right location for the right price.

But we caution any church against rushing into a facility acquisition or re-development project without the right information or understanding. Below are some pros and cons about the locality of a big box church.

Pros of the big box church

1. The spaces are generally arranged with lots of open areas, which means less demolition work and more flexibility.
2. The timeline to occupy them is significantly less than a new build. Occupancy could occur within months as opposed to years relative to constructing a new building.
3. Most of these locations have giant parking lots, a particularly important benefit for churches in urban areas with limited options for expansion.
4. Good road frontage and accessibility: In most cases the reason these facilities were developed for retail was for the traffic count, accessibility, and visibility.
5. These locations—on average— require a much lower initial cost of entry.
6. If you choose to rent, then the payments are usually lower than the interest you would pay on a loan.
7. Good street signage potential.
8. Developers are motivated to fill up their large empty spaces and will often finance the retro-fitting of the facility.
9. Developers are generally responsible for the maintenance and repair of common areas including the exterior walls and roof.

10. You can move out after the lease term...no strings attached.

Cons of the big box church

1. You must take into consideration what is often referred to as an "occupancy classification." Churches are generally classified as an assembly occupancy, which has a very different set of building code implications than a retail classification.

2. Sprinklers: In municipalities that have adopted the International Building Code, automatic fire sprinklers are required for an occupancy exceeding 300 people. If you intend to use loose seating, such as metal stackable chairs, then you determine your occupancy on a formula of seven square feet per person. So, if you have a space that is at least 2,101 square feet in the worship space, you are over the 300 threshold and thus must add a fire sprinkler system (2,101 square feet / 7 square feet = 300.1 people). And even if the room contains an existing sprinkler system, then it does not necessarily mean a previous retail space will meet the code requirements that exist for a church.

3. Big box locations often come with HVAC requirements, specifically the "CFM per person" in assembly occupancies often far exceed that of a retail store (CFM stands for "cubic feet per minute" and is a measure of air flow, often used to describe the capabilities of heating, ventilation, and air conditioning systems). You may have to add some units or totally replace the existing systems.

4. While many big box locations have ample parking, some do not have enough parking. Check with your local code office, but most likely you will need one parking space for every three to four seats. Using this example, if you have a 3:1 ratio requirement for parking, you will need 100 parking spaces, which will consume about 1.5 acres of land. Ideally a church needs 1:1.5 ratio of parking spaces to seats. A 300 seat auditorium would require 200 parking spaces on 3 acres.

5. Joint tenant issues: If you are in a strip center, you may have to limit noise, parking times, and service times to accommodate other tenants.

6. In a leased space, you don't own it, so you have to get permission to make any substantive changes to the facility.
7. In a leased space, you don't own it, so you are not building equity.
8. Again, in a leased space you don't own it, so you are accountable to a landlord.
9. Most likely, any big box space you require will come with upfit costs, and you may have to borrow money for these improvements. ...Many banks, however, are not eager to lend to a church (or any organization) that does not have an equity position in the collateral.

There are advantages to a big box location, but to make it work for a church, leaders must do their homework to minimize inevitable problems that come with these locations. One of the best ways I (Tim) can demonstrate these pros and cons is through a case study.

Let's use Elevation Church, one of the fastest-growing churches in America. Their growth is certainly exceptional, but with this growth comes even greater space challenges. Clearly, each church is different. God uses a myriad of churches to build His kingdom. Even if the scale of this project is larger than what you might consider for your church, however, the principles behind these location solutions will be helpful. In short, there is a lot to learn from churches like Elevation.

If you are not familiar with Elevation, then allow me to share a few details so you can get acquainted with the church. This Elevation campus is located in Matthews, NC within the greater Charlotte area. It was built in 2009. The location was a former 43,000 square foot retail space in a shopping center on a six-lane highway near a major interstate loop. What was once a K-Mart, then a furniture distribution warehouse, became a church.

Elevation signed a 12-year lease (five years, with another five-year option and another two-year option). The lease rate is $22,000 per month. The church spent approximately $4.6 million on tenant improvements. There were several benefits to the location of this campus, including the following attributes:

1. Lots of parking and site lighting.
2. Great road frontage and visibility.
3. Loading docks for ease of equipment and stage set loading.
4. Motivated sub-lessor.

5. Fire sprinkler riser in place.
6. Building was in the target market/ministry focus demographic of the church...only a few miles from their previous location in a school.

The site did not come without challenges, though. The church had to overcome several hurdles with the site, including these problems:

1. The center was being used by other retail tenants so service times had to be negotiated.
2. All the exterior modifications required the approval of the shopping center owners, including the name of their facility. The owners specifically requested "church" be left off their signage.
3. The structural columns were not ideal for a worship space. In the end, a couple actually had to be relocated.
4. The entire facility needed to be gutted to the base walls. Nothing was reusable except the exterior walls and the roof.

Given these hurdles, you might wonder why the church decided on this location. Why not a permanent location on land they owned?

They had specific reasons why the pros outweighed the cons:

1. The construction time at the big box location was only about four months as compared with 12-16 months for a permanent location.

2. During construction, weather was never a concern because the shell was already up and all the site work was in place.

3. The location was in an area where raw land was not available at anything close to a reasonable price.

4. The initial investment was significantly less than a new build

5. The big box location offered flexibility. Since the lease was only for five years, with the options to take it to 12 years, the church could change direction at several milestones without having to sell property.

6. Finally, the cost of rent was actually less than the cost of interest on a loan for the same period of time. We have heard people argue against leasing because of the lack of equity. Some believe leasing is like throwing money away. In some cases, that may be correct. But would you agree that interest paid on a loan is just as much a "waste" of funds as renting? It is for a

church! There is no tax benefit like there is for your home mortgage interest. So paying interest is just about the same as paying rent.

Let me show how the numbers played out. We have developed a theoretical building project budget making several assumptions on the cost of land in a similar location, cost of construction, soft costs, site development, and so on. What would it have cost Elevation to move forward with new construction?

- Land cost for about 10 acres: $2 million
- Site development (including grading, landscaping, utilities, lighting, etc.): $2.2 million
- Design and engineering (including architectural, structural, mechanical, acoustical, etc.): $475,000
- Soft costs (including permits, closing costs, surveys, etc.): $90,000
- System infrastructures (including AVL, IT, etc.): $200,000
- Construction (43,000 @ $125 per square foot): $5,400,000
- Contingency (3% to 5%): $300,000

- Construction Interest (assuming an $8.5 million loan at 5%): $220,000
- Total development costs: $10,885,000

If you look at a mortgage payment, based on a 20-year amortization schedule at 5% to 5.5% interest, in comparison to the rent, you would pay $3,358,993 in interest over the same 12 years compared with $3,168,000 in rent. When you factor in the interest paid on the short-term loan for the renovations, the amount of rent and short-term interest would be about the same as the long-term interest on a mortgage. In addition, you would still owe over $6 million on the loan.

Another way to evaluate this decision is to look at the monthly cash flow. The rent above was $22,000 per month, plus a loan on a portion of the renovation at about $20,000 per month. But the mortgage payment would be close to $59,600 per month.

While a portion of the mortgage payment is principle, the difference in monthly payments is significant. In short, the big box location costs about $42,000 per month while a new location would cost almost $60,000 per month, a significant difference when it comes to monthly cash flow! In fact, it's almost 30% more expensive to build a new campus in this case.

Every church situation is different. No cookie-cutter solution exists, even in this book. The above example worked out well for Elevation. The big box may not be right for your church. But the point we are attempting to make includes these two major themes. First, don't assume that you have to *own* or *build* a facility to have a productive ministry. Second, don't assume that you have to *own* or *build* a facility to be a wise steward of the resources God has entrusted to you.

CHAPTER SEVEN

There Goes the Neighborhood

Some almost panic when they hear of a church moving into the big box space in the local shopping center. The thoughts are almost inevitable with some:

The shopping center must be in financial trouble.

Will the church be a distraction to people?

If you thought traffic was bad before the church moved in, just wait.

I bet the whole place gets plastered with church flyers.

Real churches have their own buildings. Who are they?

While we do not want to downplay those who may have legitimate concerns about a church tenant in what was designed to be a retail space, we have found most of these concerns are exaggerated.

Recently, we conducted a survey to find answers for landlords, real estate brokers, property managers, tenants, and neighbors. Let's return to our case study.

We had the opportunity to work with Elevation Church to conduct a survey of local businesses in the immediate proximity of two Elevation Church campuses. We wanted to see how the occupancy of Elevation Church, in their two business-oriented locations (one in a shopping center and one in an office development) impacted the local merchants.

In order to prevent as much bias as possible, we structured and sent the surveys from our building company and not from Elevation Church. The survey cards were returned to my attention and then we disseminated the data. No spin or filtering.

What we found was encouraging. In fact, we believe that this data may help other churches in their quest to secure a lease or purchase of commercial properties. The survey showed that the impact was positive and did not have an adverse effect on the businesses. In fact, the biggest surprise was how positively the church was viewed. Here is what we learned from these businesses since Elevation Church opened in their community:

1. Approximately 70% of all issued surveys were completed and returned.
2. Of the respondents, 81% were restaurants or some type of food service.
3. 87% indicated that they had experienced an increase in customer traffic.
4. Almost 90% reported an increase in sales.
5. Over 85% told us that they had seen an increase in repeat customers.
6. And best of all, 0% reported any adverse impact on their business since the church moved in.

Obviously, every community, section of town, business types, business mix, church, and local government can impact these types of results, but the above survey would indicate that the locality of a church in a commerce center can be an asset to the congregation (by being in the center of culture and the community) but also the community and its businesses.

CHAPTER EIGHT

The Economic Value of a Church: A Surprising Reality

Many churches looking to impact their communities through multisite locations or church planting are often faced with the dilemma of not just identifying a suitable place to meet, but also being able to navigate issues associated with the local governmental authorities.

This is particularly true when searching for space in an urban environment or where a facility is currently on the tax rolls. Many cities only see tax revenue that a property can generate and get their feathers ruffled when an organization might threaten their income stream. This is too often the case with politicians that are not familiar with the study of economics as well as the "cause and effect" of industries, businesses, and other organizations to the overall economic impact.

If you have ever lived in a community that was thinking about a professional sports franchise, you have undoubtedly heard the pundits talk about all the tax breaks the city is providing the ownership group, coupled with a retort as to the incredible economic benefit the new stadium or arena will bring to the region. Hotels reservation increase. Visitors will use the airport. Traffic will increase in restaurants and bars. Other organizations will rent the arena for non-sporting events.

Well, what about a church? What is its economic impact on a community? Most do not pay any form of taxes, property or sales tax. So how can it help your community economically? All they do is ask for donations.

As we have been compiling research for this book we found some very interesting data that was compiled to quantify the economic value that a church brings to a community. A couple years ago, a University of Pennsylvania professor and a national secular research group based in Center City Philadelphia took up that seemingly unanswerable question: What is a church's economic worth?

With a list they devised of 54 value categories, they attempted to calculate the economic "halo effect" of a dozen religious congregations in Philadelphia: 10 Protestant churches, a Catholic parish, and a synagogue.

They added up the money generated by weddings and funerals, festivals, counseling programs, preschools, and elder care. They tallied the salaries of staff and the wages of roofers, plumbers, even snow shovelers. They put dollar signs on intangibles, too, such as helping people find work and teaching children to be socially responsible. They even measured the diameter of trees on church campuses. The grand total for the 12 congregations was staggering: $50,577,098 in annual economic benefits.

These are very interesting assumptions with a fresh perspective for city officials to consider when evaluating whether or not to allow a church to move into an otherwise tax-producing property. But how do you get this point across to the city leaders? How do you get them to understand your case?

Given the above research, as well as our own experiences with hundreds of churches across the country, your first step may be to send a letter to a city official that you believe you either have access to or have an influencer in your circle of influence that can make an introduction for you. To help you get started, below is an example of a letter one pastor sent to the mayor in the town where he wanted to launch a multisite campus.

Dear Mr./Mrs. Official:

Greetings from YOUR CHURCH. I hope this note finds you doing well and enjoying the challenges of the job. It's my hope YOUR CITY flourishes on your watch!

I am writing in hopes of getting fifteen minutes of your time. I'd like to discuss YOUR CHURCH expanding into YOUR CITY.

YOUR CHURCH began nearly X years ago with X people meeting in the living room of a home. Today over X people are involved, with an average weekly attendance of over X. Three years ago we opened a second site in another part of YOUR CITY. We are now prayerfully considering a third location. Given the X number of YOUR CITY families who are involved at YOUR CHURCH, we are hoping to locate in or near another part of YOUR CITY. We believe this would be a good thing for them and for the city.

Why would I boldly suggest that it would be a win for YOUR CITY to take even more land off the tax base? Because vibrant churches make a catalytic difference in their communities, and that is the kind of church we strive to be.

Members at YOUR CHURCH serve. Last year those who attend YOUR CHURCH not only contributed X service hours through church programs, they also donated close to X volunteer hours in YOUR CITY through community programs. We would love to see the number of volunteer hours expand. In fact, our strategic plan calls for the number of community service hours to grow to X amount over the next six years.

We challenge men to raise their game. Each Friday morning close to X men show up at 6 AM for a high impact gathering that's part sports bar and part church. Over the course of ninety minutes they are encouraged to be better men, better husbands, fathers, employers, employees, neighbors, and friends. Why do we target men? Because men enjoy an outsized influence in the world. When they thrive those around them thrive, and when they fail they pull others down with them. We are anxious to expand this program into YOUR CITY.

We focus on families. YOUR CHURCH works to help families thrive. We do this in a variety of ways: workshops for parents, support groups for new moms, etc. Close to X people attend ministry programs at the church, and over the last three years these programs have moved into the public schools. The students, parents, teachers, and administrators love it. We are anxious to bring these ministries into YOUR CITY.

We bring practical help. Sometimes the help people need is tangible. They need someone to clean their gutters, repair a broken door, or fix a window. YOUR CHURCH has teams that provide free minor home repair to those who attend YOUR CHURCH and those who do not. Typically the ones being helped are single moms and the elderly. Sometimes the help people need is financial. Our benevolence ministry has been quietly helping people pay bills, secure car repairs, and move out of crisis mode since the day the church began.

I could go on. We host support groups for those struggling with grief or moving through divorce. We offer our facilities rent free to groups like AA. We hold free concerts. Suffice it to say, we are a church that is trying to make a positive difference.

So why am I telling you this? Why am I selling so hard? Why am I asking for your help? Because so far we have been unable to secure a site that works. A team from the church has been looking for some months. They explored several dozen locations before recommending an area in YOUR CITY. Subsequently, we've spent some time trying to be a part of the redevelopment of property and explored other options as well. The ideal solution appears to be a building that had been vacant for over ten years, but it is zoned in ways that prevent us from moving forward.

We believe we would be a great fit for this facility and are anxious to move forward. When I shared this with an influencer in YOUR CITY, he encouraged me to write directly to you.

I will call in a day or two to see if it's possible to meet. I'd like to hear about your vision for YOUR CITY. I'd like to explore ways we might help be a part of bringing that vision to life, and I'd like to ask for your help in securing X property.

Thanks for reading this.

Press On,

Pastor, YOUR CHURCH

By the way, the mayor of this actual example responded favorably and went to work in helping the church secure the desired facility. This is what he said to the pastor, "Look, I love what you want to do. We want and need churches. If this is the building you want, let's go make this happen."

CHAPTER NINE

A Sense of Place in the Rented Space

Most of us can gain a sense of story by walking into Westminster Abbey. The history of great people defines the building. Monuments and statues mark important moments in Western history. But can a multisite church or church plant tell a story through their rented space in a strip mall? Should the church even attempt to tell this story? Does it really matter if a big box church doesn't create a sense of place in the rented space? We believe it is worth the mental, emotional, and financial investment to communicate a unique story. In fact every church—big box or cathedral, owned, or rented—should tell a story.

Why does it matter? Because stories impact people. Stories appeal or repel. They make an impression mentally and emotionally. And buildings tell a story. If you own or have a long-term lease it is easier to tell your story, but you can tell your story even in short-term rented facilities. You can impact the exterior elevation (in most cases) and the interior environments. You can theme the rooms, change colors and add lighting to communicate your story that these kinds of facilities present.

But what if you are in a school, community center, performing arts center, YMCA, or any other facility that you rent and only have access to one day a week? What if you are in the building for only a few hours at a time? Are you stuck with what they give you? Do you have to settle with the decor, features, and storytelling of that facility? Are you relegated to compromising on every aspect of the environment and sense of place? You are not.

Any facility, rented or owned, short-term or long-term can be transformed into a warm and inviting church environment that tells your story your way. We see it happening every week in urban, suburban, and rural communities. Let's think about all of the different ways you tell your story through your church locality.

Website. Your website is the new front porch. It should invite people in like a well-made front porch. There are lots of different types of front porches, so make it relevant and contextual to your neighborhood. Like a home on a street, your website must match your community.

Streetscape. Just because you cannot change the façade of the high school you are renting does not mean that you should neglect the sense of arrival. Just because you only have the facility one day of the week does not mean that you should just settle for what the existing built environment communicates. Add banners. Install temporary signs. Add bright colors that catch people's attention. Use digital effects. Line the street with people in matching t-shirts. Make a visual statement. Don't squander this opportunity to catch the attention of the community and suck them in. They may not pull in the parking lot the first time they drive by, but if you are consistent and persistent, they are more likely to become your guest.

Parking ministry. Parking is one of the most overlooked ministries in churches today. Much potential exists, but few churches tell a story by making an impression as people get out of their cars. It does not matter if you own the parking lot or are just renting, you can impact guests by giving them a pleasant experience starting in the parking lot. Get them talking positively about your church before they put their car in park. Research demonstrates first impressions happen within seven seconds, which means the tone of your church's story begins with guests before they even get inside your building.

Which way do I go? As people enter the church's story, are they lost? Signage plays a bigger role than most realize. Have you ever felt tension—if not fear—in an airport because you could not find the right sign. Did that experience jade your view of the locality just because you couldn't find your way? Make it obvious. Use all of the senses to lead your guest to the entrances you want them to use. There should be visual clues at a minimum, but why not use auditory and interpersonal clues?

Write scripts. Develop and use scripts with your volunteers that depict the experience you want every guest to realize. This type of story-telling is a great way to set expectations for your volunteers and to train them as you continue to grow and expand your teams.

Environmental Experience. How do you make a school entrance feel like a warm and inviting lobby where people want to hangout and share life together? How do we make the kids spaces feel fun and secure? How do we downplay the institutional feel of the typical school facility? As you develop your plan, think about the mediums that communicate your culture and vision, then figure out how to make them portable. Maybe it is TV monitors that are mounted to truss material that can be stored in a travel case and pulled out on Sunday. It may be banners, a portable espresso machine, comfy couches, area rugs, banners, or static applied graphics. It may also mean being a partner. You can think outside the box in a big box church.

Personal Interactions. A building can be perfect, but without personal interaction, it is just a building. No building alone can create a sense of community. Not even the most elegant cathedral defines a community without the people assembling in it. And nothing overcomes a less-than-ideal environment like engaging personal interactions. There are many obvious human touch points that will impact your guests. From the parking lot to the entry area, your greeters set first impressions in stone. Are signs informative or confusing? Do your volunteers do a job or are they equipped to impact guests? These front line ambassadors are your first story-tellers in the church.

Don't succumb to the trap of mediocrity just because you rent a school or other facility. Expend the same intentionality (if not more) that you would if you owned a facility. You don't have to settle. Your church story is important. Tell it.

CHAPTER TEN

Eternity Begins in the Parking Lot: The Seven-Second Introduction

How much time do you have to make a first impression on a guest; seven seconds. That's it. Some experts say a little more; some say a little less. But the average first impression occurs within seven seconds. It's not much time before impressions about your church begin to settle into the mind of a guest.

You must invest in these first seven seconds. It's not much time to impact the thought and emotional reaction of guests. Every touch point during a guest experience has the opportunity to build on the previous interaction, or to destroy it. Every encounter and milestone of this first experience is critical, like a set of building blocks. Without a strong foundation, the rest of the blocks find themselves less stable.

Assuming your first-time guest has made the conscious decision to pull onto your site, their first seven-second encounter will be in your parking lot. A guest's first impression starts at the entrance of the parking lot and may continue until they reach your front door. Too often church leaders think the parking lot is irrelevant and just a place to store the means of transportation used by the congregation. They see it as just common place instead of a touch point and a place to impact people (thus souls). Don't make the mistake of neglecting the parking lot!

As you think about your parking experience, below are three things that are foundational in making the first seven seconds the best you can.

Have a Parking Ministry

This is a great way to accomplish two significant ministry initiatives for two very different groups. The first group it impacts is obvious...the guest. A vibrant, proactive, enthusiastic, and welcoming group of people can lift your spirits and defuse some of the anxiety that a guest may be experiencing. Seeing happy people waving, smiling, even acting spontaneous has more impact on others than you realize.

The second group that this ministry impacts is your team. Many of the churches we serve have met in schools or other temporary facilities for years, and now they have a facility in which to meet. During those years of being a "church in the box," they set up teams that would show up on Saturday night or Sunday morning at the crack of dawn to prepare for the worship that day. These people have developed a bond and a kinship that is infectious. The setup team has actually become their "small group" and they love doing life together. But what happens when you do not need to setup every week? What do these people do?

We have been on set up teams with people that were not yet Christ-followers and others that are new followers and others that are more comfortable doing physical labor. To not provide a similar ministry opportunity once you occupy a new space that does not require setup robs them of a ministry opportunity that brings them passion. By starting or expanding a parking ministry, you open up a new opportunity for many of these people to serve. This applies to temporary facilities and permanent facilities. We have to park somewhere.

See the First Seven Seconds as a Ministry and Not a Mundane Task

Do not use the parking ministry as just a functional activity but rather an opportunity to impact people's lives. And if you believe that prayer is impactful, then your parking team should be praying for each of the cars entering the lot. The parking lot should be blanketed with praying people; it should be the largest prayer chapel on your campus. Help set the tone for your guests' experiences through a parking lot ministry and see what happens.

Function and Safety

Church parking lots are not like a retail center, even though many designers and civil engineers lay them out as if they were. In a retail or other commercial application, most of the vehicular traffic is spread out over the entire day. Cars pull off and pull on at different times during the day. But a church parking lot is more similar to an event venue...more like a concert venue or theme park or sports complex. You have a lot of cars trying to enter and/or exit the site at the same time.

And if you have back-to-back worship experiences with 15 minutes or less between services, you have a real issue. Having a succinct plan for how to best get cars on and off your site will reduce the amount of stress for the drivers, but will also provide a safer environment. If drivers are not attempting to navigate the parking lot on their own, the likelihood of mishaps is greatly reduced. And not just for vehicular traffic, but for pedestrian.

Please do not view your sea of asphalt as just a place to park vehicles but be intentional and make it a safe environment that is bathed in prayer and enhances the experience of your guests. Those first seven seconds matter, perhaps for eternity.

CHAPTER ELEVEN

What Would Jesus Negotiate?

A few years ago, *Inc.* Magazine published an article on how to negotiate a good deal on a lease. The tactics in the article were a bit more mercenary than most churches would be comfortable with, but the concepts were helpful. Churches exist to make disciples, to help people become more like Jesus. The lease negotiation tactics are not recorded in the New Testament. Given that churches should reflect Christ in all they do, how can a congregation approach a lease negotiation in a way that honors Jesus? We can incorporate some of the business concepts of the *Inc.* article with Christ-like attitude and negotiate in a way that brings glory to God.

Be transparent and Set the Terms

No church should be sneaky in a negotiation over a lease. But there is nothing wrong with attempting to do what is in the best interest of the congregation. In fact, most landlords will expect every tenant to negotiate terms. You don't have to take the first offer, but don't resort to underhanded tactics under the guise of stewardship.

Your first order of business is to negotiate the term, or duration, of the lease and the rent you will pay, which is usually figured per square foot. Leases typically include an option to renew at the end of the term, at either a specified rent or prevailing market conditions.

Short-term leases (1-3 years) offer the flexibility of minimalizing the risks if the church doesn't do well or outgrows the facility. Long term leases (5-15 years) offer the best return on the build-out investment and usually result in better lease rates with the landlord. Generally, our recommendation is to negotiate a long-term contract of 10-15 years that is renewable in 3-5 year increments.

Be flexible, Count the Cost...and Count the Square Footage

Don't expect to get a better-than-market rate just because you're a church. Commercial properties are generally valued according to the square-foot rental rates in lease contracts. As a result, landlords like to hold firm on the contracted monthly rates, even while they offer rebates off the monthly rent.

Of course, as far as you are concerned, a deal is a deal, no matter its structure -- at least in the short term. Measure the space before you sign a lease. Spaces have sometimes been reconfigured three or four times, and often they're going off an old floor plan that is not accurate. Also, determine if there is some common area that is not within your lease space that you are paying for in addition to the actual usable space. Be reasonable, but also do your homework.

Be Detailed and Gracious

Landlords tend to pass on expenses to their tenants, one way or another. In a triple net, or NNN, lease, the landlord bills separately for taxes (something a church has to pay the landlord as the landlord is not tax exempt), insurance, and operating expenses or common area maintenance (CAM). In a multi-tenant complex, expenses are prorated among tenants according to their share of the total space. CAM is usually broadly defined. Besides upkeep for shared facilities such as the parking lot, lobby, stairwells, and restrooms, it can also include virtually any operating expense.

Watch these details. Be aware of which expenses your landlord will bill, particularly as part of CAM. Utilities are also the responsibility of the tenant. In shopping centers, tenants are metered individually. In most office buildings, utility costs are apportioned by square footage.

Most landlords attempt to hold tenants responsible for maintenance and repairs of anything other than the roof, exterior walls, and parking lots. Some require renters to replace failing equipment, including the heating, ventilation, and air conditioning systems, a potentially enormous outlay. If the building is approaching 10 years old, or the HVAC systems have seen inordinate use, get the HVAC systems inspected, along with the plumbing and electrical equipment. If you find problems, make it a point of negotiation. As you negotiate with a potential landlord, be gracious. But do not use grace as an excuse to neglect the details.

Steward the Big Rocks

Leases almost always favor the landlord. But you can build in clauses that level the playing field. Be strategic in setting priorities. Don't try to make comprehensive changes, as they will most likely turn the negotiations in the wrong direction and sour the deal. Be more concerned with making four or five important changes than dozens of small changes. What are some big rocks to note?

Negotiate on these important pieces of the lease arrangement.

Co-tenancy: Many shopping centers and office/warehouse complexes rely on big anchor stores to draw traffic. So what happens to the smaller tenants when an anchor closes its doors? A co-tenancy clause lets a renter escape the lease if the landlord doesn't replace the anchor in a specified period.

Personal guaranty: Many landlords will insist on a personal guaranty from the tenant. We recommend that you make every effort to avoid this guaranty. Consider other options, but do not put the lead pastor, elders, deacons, trustees or board at personal risk if at all possible.

Sublease: A sublease allows a tenant to sublet space to another organization. A sublease allows you to turn your fixed costs into variable costs, especially if you need to vacate all or part of the space.

Working with Brokers

You may have recruited your broker, but your broker isn't necessarily working for you. He is working for the landlord who pays the commission, which in most markets is from 5 percent to 6 percent of the total lease value, split between the landlord's listing agent and the broker who introduced you to the property. If you use a broker make sure he represents you, understands church facility needs and owes his fiduciary duty to you. Here are other things to keep in mind about brokers:

Listen to your lawyer. A good real estate lawyer— who really does work for you—can recommend brokers who will advise you in good faith.

Trust but verify. Be careful to not lean too heavily on your broker when it comes time to negotiate. Many brokers will do whatever it takes to get the deal signed and don't want to add complexity. Make sure your broker is negotiating the best deal possible for the church. All contract details should cross your lawyer's desk.

CHAPTER TWELVE

When Your Church Meets in a Movie Theater

Mark Batterson is the lead pastor of National Community Church in Washington DC. They may be considered the pioneer at doing church in movie theaters. In fact, their website address is www.theaterchurch.com.

After a prayer walk around Capitol Hill, God opened an amazing door of opportunity for National Community to hold services in the movie theaters at Union Station. On September 21, 2003, they launched their second location in the Ballston Common Mall movie theaters just over the river in Northern Virginia from their original site.

Doing church in the middle of the marketplace had become part of their DNA, and they began dreaming of new ways for the church and community to intersect daily.

By October 2009, National Community had launched services at movie theaters in

Georgetown and Kingstowne. Then, Pastor Mark got a phone call that the Union Station movies theaters would be closing immediately. Their three Sunday services at Union Station had nowhere to go, so they crammed into the performance level of their coffee shop, Ebenezer's, for what they hoped would be a temporary solution.

Over the next few years National Community launched their fifth and sixth locations at the movie theaters at Potomac Yard in Northern Virginia and in Northwest DC at the GALA Theatre.

Movie theaters for many churches like National Community have become the new cathedrals of today. They are in the heart of communities. The screen is the new stained glass. While the downsides of such space exist, these localities can be a tremendous way to do church right in the midst of your community.

Several lessons emerge from choosing the locality of a movie theater as the sanctuary for your congregation. Our society is moving away towards modernity and towards a postmodern mindset. The monolithic ideals of previous generations are giving way to a plurality of relative deals. The church building was once viewed as a default destination. People gravitated towards the building because it was a church. So previous generations made church buildings look like what people expected in a church.

People no longer naturally gravitate towards the church campus, so the church must go to the people. Theater churches can help a congregation leverage the location. What was once an impossible thought—*our church is meeting in a theater near you*—has not only become a reality, but also a strategy for reaching people.

CHAPTER THIRTEEN

Funding Multiple Locations in a Tough Economy

by Brad Leeper

Multisite and multi-venue options are the new normal. No question. Given the new non-normal economic metrics, however, funding the multisite or multi-venue confounds the best of leadership teams.

How might churches consider gathering increased funds for expansion? Additional funding can be secured if leaders know how to pursue the alignment of the vision and the hearts of your people. To understand how to secure your funding, understand what is going on in the current giving patterns.

First, general giving for missional churches tends to be healthy. Churches that have a focused vision and can articulate that vision in the midst of fruitfulness generally are up in their giving. While there are some exceptions to this trend, most churches have weathered the storm and have done much better than predicted in their regular giving.

Second, bank loans are very hard to obtain. Churches found an all-too-easy marketplace for loans until the recession that began in 2008. Lenders have rebounded by enforcing much more stringent requirements to get a loan for any kind of expansion. Being debt-free is not even considered an advantage. Banks are now looking for cash reserves, excess cash flow, and increased cash participation by a church in the project for loan consideration.

Third, people will give sacrificially for your expansion project, but their questions are more demanding and their process more cautious. The better you make the case for the expansion and align the expansion to the heart of the donor, the better the results. Extra giving is in correlation to the mission critical nature of the project. The process of project giving is much, much more complex than ever. Be aware, however, that the overall project giving results are much lower than the unusually bountiful years prior to the recession.

Fourth, the donor is more cautious about your project. Still open, yes, but more cautious in the process. Surprisingly, some churches still presume upon the donor because, from the leadership perspective, the project makes a compelling case for everyone to give. Presumption and poor communication will doom your giving totals. People seem to have generally concluded that we have weathered the hardest hit from the recession and it will probably not get worse. The donor, however, is not convinced that it will get better anytime soon.

The shorter the duration of the giving season for the project, the more inclined the donor is to give generously. It is easier for people to give above and beyond for 12 months than 36 months. They are simply not as confident about 36 months out.

Fifth, higher capacity donors remain in play. While many have suffered through this season, a smaller group has done well financially. As highlighted in Esther, God has placed a group of people in play for such a time as this. Knowing the new dialog to converse with this group is the challenge. And yes, you probably have a group of these people in your church. Nearly all churches do. Often, leaders do not know that they are there. And just as often, this group does not appear in your list of top givers.

Sixth, giving to projects is more sacrificial than ever. People will take you seriously when you make a case for your expansion or multisite. Even when they are already making adjustments in their personal lifestyle, they will sacrifice financially to make the expansion a reality.

Simply be aware that their giving really means something deep to them. The giving is not from surplus. We in leadership must honor their love for God and the church by not asking them to give to a project that is not mission critical.

Churches do have options for raising funds to expand to multiple locations. First, some churches can absorb a multisite or venue from their general budgets. Although this option is not as common, it is an option if a church has substantial cash reserves and believes that the multisite can be self-sustaining quickly.

Second, depending on the church size and history with offerings, a one-time church-wide offering can generate substantial funds. The communication for this option, however, is far more complex than ever. A one-time offering is not a simple exercise. Layers of communication tailored to various groups in the church are essential for success.

Increasingly, project giving is designated for non-capital expenditures. It is not unusual to ask a church body to fund a multisite over a period of time with over and above giving. Do not exceed 12 months and try to keep the giving season as short as possible.

Additionally, multisite and other expansion options tend to make a compelling case to higher capacity donors. Their mindset is much different than that of a typical donor. They more often value getting involved in projects that are compelling and where they as a donor can do things that few other people can do. This option is often my first consideration in working with a church in a multisite or multi-venue expansion.

Most multisite churches are launched with a core team and campus pastor leading up to the public introduction. As a challenge to the core, consider asking them to include extra giving designated to the project. As you might guess, financial involvement is an excellent indicator of being all in for the project. Would you want to go into battle with people unwilling to give toward the project?

Given the complexity of the giving environment, a combination of the above factors is more often employed to fund a project. The challenge is to know how to pace each of these areas and to communicate with excellence to the various groups. Leadership cannot pull this off with a flippant plan and without careful planning over a longer period of time. The entire process of raising project funds is much longer than ever. What are some other considerations in launching a multisite church? In working with many churches using multisite, these questions stand out as critical:

When will leadership expect the multisite to be self-sustaining financially?

This value must be determined early in the strategy planning.

Will we make the campus pastors responsible for generosity and stewardship in their leadership?

Some campus pastors do not embrace this value and believe that the senior pastor alone is responsible for generosity. The stronger the campus in giving, the more likely the success of the campus. Place the value of generosity high on the campus pastor's responsibility. Only hire campus pastors that can passionately see generosity as part of their roles.

Does the senior pastor still carry the primary load in vision casting and resourcing?

Yes, and increasingly so. Many of my clients tell me how reluctant they are to lead in this area. After working on their project and engaging with their people, they often report the time as the best they have had in ministry for years. The senior visionary leader has more direct impact in giving than any other factor after the mission critical nature of the project.

Does senior leadership's and the senior pastor's giving remain important for any expansion project?

The speed of leadership always impacts the speed of the team. If you as leaders are considering an expansion project like multisite, expect to lead the way in bountiful giving. If you are not willing to invest financially in a sacrificial amount for the project, do not move forward with the project. That expansion is doomed for failure and there is likely a disconnect with the mission critical nature of the project.

CHAPTER FOURTEEN

Making Sure the First Month Goes Well

by Rich Birch

When launching a new location, visible victories in the first month are critical. Before the big "grand opening" of your next multisite campus you need to host a series of soft launch Sundays. These services are designed to get all your teams and systems ready before you cut the ribbon. I've been involved in a bunch of these over the last 10+ years of launching multisite campuses. Allow me to share with you some essential advice for making your next soft launch Sundays go well.

Under Promise...Over Deliver

Every time you talk about these services you need to stress with your people that these are "rehearsal" services ... that your team will stop the service to fix whatever needs to be fixed. Stress that you are doing this to make everything perfect for their friends at the grand opening. But you need to work to ensure that the services are a close to perfect as possible ... do some extra band rehearsals ... practice your hosting spots ... work hard to make it great. Lowering your people's expectations and then over-delivering on the experience will boost their confidence in inviting friends to the grand opening.

Do More

How many weekends of practice services do you think you need? Do twice as many! There is no downside to getting it right before launch Sunday. You don't want your people wondering if there are going to be any problems on that day. I find that three or four weeks of soft launch services is a sweet spot for most churches.

Who are you inviting to Grand Opening?

This question needs to be on the tip of the tongue of every leader as they talk with people. Talk about who you are inviting from stage ... ask people in their team huddles to talk about who they are inviting ... take time to pray for the first time guests that will be coming to the grand opening. You can't over-communicate this message. Grand openings only happen once. Leverage it as a motivation for your people to invite friends!

Structured Feedback

Make sure that you have a mechanism for getting feedback from your leaders after these services. Conference calls work great. Even an emailed survey can garner feedback from people. The goal of these services is to learn from your people what you can improve for launch Sunday.

New Every Weekend

Even though you're going to work hard to make the services great and ensure that all the equipment is onsite for the first weekend, it's nice when you can roll out new items every soft launch Sunday for people to see. Adding signage every weekend is great way to show you're making progress towards launch!

Cherish the Family Time

These services will have less people than your grand opening Sunday and the services after that. Don't get bummed by the smaller crowds Rather, embrace the chance to love on your core community. Take extra time to talk to people who you might not normally get a chance to connect with at a service. Serve a volunteer lunch one of the weekends (or every weekend!). Soak in the goodness of your community.

RECRUIT!

It will never be as easy as this time to recruit volunteers to join your teams. There will be a significant number of people who will be interested signing up to serve on a team. Don't look down on late comers. They just needed to know it was actually going to happen before they could sign up. Be positive and get them plugged into the launch effort.

Invite Cards

Make sure have lots of invite cards on hand to give to your people. I like having them bundled up in packs of 10.

In the coming weeks hundreds of new campuses will launch multisite churches across the country. The process is a lot like birthing a new baby. We are often so focused on the delivery we don't spend time thinking about what happens after the newborn arrives. The first month in the life of a multisite campus is critical. What you practice in the first month can determine whether your site fails or succeeds in the long term.

Make sure you plan out a fantastic celebration opportunity in the first few weeks. Have your core group over to you house for dinner and prepare some heartfelt words to share with the group. Take a bunch of great photos of opening day and put them into an album and hand them out. You spent a lot of time thinking about how to get these volunteers onto your team, so take a healthy amount of time to thank them for what they are doing!

Additionally, you *must* follow up with first time guests. There is a high likelihood that you will see as many first time guests in your first month as you will see in the entire next six months combined. Be ready to follow up with each and every one. Make yourself and your team available to have coffee with them. Be constantly finding ways to connect them with people in your community.

Your volunteers and leaders have been focused on the launch and will be wondering "what's next?" for your church. You need an encore. You need to promote the next big thing. Before you launch, ensure that you have something lined up to direct your people towards once the campus is open. Maybe you have a community service project planned for 6 weeks after launch, or you could be talking about the next big series coming up. Build a momentum bridge to the next big thing.

Lastly, focus on continuous improvement. From the first weekend you host services, begin to ask for and give consistent feedback on how your team can improve. Is there a way to improve the teaching experience for people? What can we do to make sure parents feel great dropping off their kids? Could the band work on the transitions between songs to make them smoother? Does what our first time guests experience present a welcoming experience for them?

Embedding the idea of constant improvement from the beginning with help drive long term improvement as a campus. You only get to do the first month once. It's critically important to go into that month with a plan to leverage it.

CHAPTER FIFTEEN

The Language of Locality

by Rich Birch

The language we use as church leaders has the potential to shape the culture of our church because it frames our thinking. Often the language we use when we launch a new ministry can set it on an unintended course simply through the way we've helped people understand it. Here are some negative language patterns I've seen present in multisite churches over the years. Avoid these patterns to give your vision the best chance to thrive!

Us vs. Them

It's dangerous to start referring to the various campuses of your church as "them" because it's starts to set up emotional walls and separates the team.

Avoid: "*They* bought some new technology this weekend at the Springfield campus."

Alternative: "*We* bought new technology for the Springfield campus this weekend."

Mothership, Headquarters, and Main Campus

Don't treat your original location with extra reverence through some sort of special name. What if you always referred to one of your kids as "the main one?"

Avoid: "Our next leadership development event is back at the mothership."

Alternative: "The training next month is at our Ritson Road Campus."

North, East, South, and West Campus Names

When people arrive at a new location and find out that this location is the "West Campus of Cool Community Church," there is a subtle message that the real thing is east of here! Also this naming scheme limits the number of campuses. Surely you're not going to have the North North East Campus!

Avoid: "Are you going to join us as the West Campus when it launches?"

Alternative: "We'd love to have you join the Stoney Creek Campus this fall!"

Unnecessarily Drawing Attention to Technology

If you use video to deliver the teaching at your campuses there is no need to point that out to people. It would be like 15 years ago standing up and saying "In just a few minutes Pastor Mike is going to use a microphone and stand on a stage with lights." We're past the place where you need to call out the technology.

Avoid: "Today our teaching is coming in via live video stream from our Chatham Campus."

Alternative: "Pastor Mike is kicking off a brand new series today!"

Language matters. How you say things matters. Words can be powerful. Choose the language of locality that helps unify and not divide.

CHAPTER SIXTEEN

Ten Rules for Managing Multiple Localities

by Rich Birch

Recently I was talking with a church leader in a multisite church. His words broke my heart. This leader was reflecting on when their central services counterpart would come and visit their campus to "help." "They just show and vomit all over our people," he mentioned. What he meant was that too much information just spewed all over his leaders and volunteers.

I've spent 10+ years in multisite churches working in various central services roles, visiting campuses to provide insight in doing church. Over that time I've made hundreds of these sorts of visits. My heart sank when this leader described their central counterpart that way, and it got me thinking about some guidelines for the way central staff need to conduct themselves when on these visits.

1. You're not that big of a deal. Really. The power dynamics are set up in a strange way to make people who come from the "central" team to appear like they are the "big-wigs coming from head office." Do everything you can to fight that perception. Be there to serve. Wear a volunteer t-shirt. Ask lots of questions. Be winsome in your communication.

2. Get the who before the what. Take time to get to know the team at the campus. Before you jump in on the tasks that you have come to accomplish at the campus make sure to connect with the team members. Learn names and try to remember information about people from visit to visit.

3. Show up regularly. Make a regular effort to be at the new location as often as you can. As you get to 3-4 campuses it becomes critical that you develop the discipline to be at a new location every weekend to ensure that you are staying as connected as possible.

4. Give the inside track to what's coming next. As a member of the central team you often have a sense of what is coming up in the future of the church. Use these site visits as a chance to spread a bit of excitement about what's coming up in the life of the church. Think of one talking point to spread before you arrive!

5. Don't forget tools and training. Every time you are on site you should be rolling out a new tool or helping with some training. Maybe you can spend some extra time with the team leaders working on a system that needs some support or you can help them with a new coaching tool for working with volunteers. Find ways to be helpful.

6. Affirm before giving advice. Make sure to have your senses tuned to pick up on what is right for each specific location. Take time to point out what is working before you jump into giving them advice about what they can fix.

7. Have a mental checklist. As much as you want to be relationally warm and open with people, you need to have a clear sense of mission for your time at the campus. Make sure you've thought through what you want to see and who you want to connect with. Please don't have a clipboard with an actual checklist. If you need a reminder you could write out a few notes on an index card and put in your back pocket.

8. Connect with the campus pastor. Make sure you take time to connect with the campus pastor when you are on site. You must give the campus pastor the authority to accomplish the responsibilities expected of the position.

9. Provide post-Sunday feedback. Loop back with the local team to give them your feedback and comments as soon after your visit as possible. Make sure to give them insights in what you experienced that were great as well as those things that need a little work on.

10. Pick your battles. Stay focused on feedback that is going to have the highest leverage of change in the campus. Nobody enjoys a laundry list of 25 things they need to change.

The goal of your visit is that people will look forward to the next time you are at their campus. It's not about fixing every item this time around but building trust with the team and adding value so they will want to have you come again. Senior leaders should aim for long-term team development not short-term system compliance.

CHAPTER SEVENTEEN

Go Forth and Multiply

When Jesus said to the disciples "I will build my church" (Matthew 16:18), he was not referring to bricks and mortar but about flesh and blood. Our human nature wants to build something tangible as an act of worship. Peter's response on the Mt. of Transfiguration when Moses and Elijah appeared with Jesus is the typical human reaction, *"Let's put up three shelters—one for you, one for Moses and one for Elijah"* (Luke 9:33).

Jesus was talking about a spiritual kingdom comprised of his followers who will expand his kingdom by proclaiming good news and performing good works in his name. The church is not a building. The church is people. Jesus did not say, "Go build a building." He said, "Build my church." There is a big difference.

Though the church is a universal and spiritual reality, it also has a visible and physical expression. Whenever those followers get together in His name, they meet in a *place.* They are the *ecclesia* "assembly," a tangible expression of the body of Christ. This place becomes sacred space not because of location or architecture but because Jesus is present with them in a spiritual and corporate sense.

The early followers of Jesus began the habit of meeting regularly together on the first day of the week (Sunday) to commemorate the fact that Jesus rose from the dead on the first day of the week. They met to worship, to be instructed, to pray, to break bread together, and collect offerings to help the poor and spread the good news (1 Corinthians 16:2).

They met in buildings—temple courts, homes, market-places, synagogues, schools, and even underground cemeteries called catacombs. Eventually they constructed buildings and built large cathedrals.

Buildings have always played a role in the building of Jesus' church. Buildings are not the primary goal, but they do serve a purpose. This is what this book is about. It's about being good stewards and making the best use of these places where visible communities of faith gather. How we *do church* in public places of worship equips us to go back into the world to *be the church*.

We believe that the mandate of every church, church plant, and multisite campus is found in Matthew 28. These words are the final words of Jesus to His disciples after He completed His mission on earth. These words are the marching orders for the Church. It is His Great Commission to us:

> *Therefore, go and make disciples of all the nations, baptizing them in the name of the Father and the Son and the Holy Spirit. Teach these new disciples to obey all the commands I have given you. And be sure of this: I am with you always, even to the end of the age. (NLT)*

We also believe that God desires every church, church plant, and multisite campus to be a blessing, to be fruitful and multiply. We believe it is God's will for every church to be a reproducing church. From the very beginning God created every living organism to be a blessing and to reproduce. This is the divine DNA that God breathed into every living thing He created. We believe this includes every living expression of the Body of Christ.

*And God **blessed** them, and God said unto them, "Be **fruitful,** and **multiply**. . ." Genesis 1:28 (KJV)*

God wants to bless your church so it will be a blessing to your community. Healthy, living things are fruitful and reproduce. It's God's desire that your church be fruitful and reproduce. Every church, and your church, is divinely designed to be a blessing, to be fruitful and multiply.

Fruitful and reproducing churches will have to deal with the issue of "space" at some point. They will build, buy, or rent buildings. They will go multisite and/or plant new churches. That is what multiplying churches do. Being prudent in how you address your physical space needs will be a critical part of your ministry.

It is an exciting time to be "doing church." There are many resources and organizations in place to help you succeed. We trust that you will use this book to be the best steward possible in considering the right tool to multiply your church ministry.

But keep in mind these critical aspects of physical space. The church building is only a tool to help you reach your ministry objectives, vision, and mission. It will never save a soul.

Buildings don't reach people, people reach people. Facilities, in general, will be the second largest line item in your annual budget behind personnel costs.

So be wise.

Be diligent.

Be prudent.

Seek wise counsel.

Go forth and multiply!

The Advantages of Disadvantages of Non-Traditional Space

The following section will provide you will a quick reference guide as to some of the advantages and disadvantages of the most common facilities that church planters and multisite churches consider when expanding.

No locality is perfect.

The list below will help you understand the benefits and challenges of common choices for new locations.

Schools

Advantages

- Location is generally within your target market.
- Ample parking, unless it is an elementary school.

- High schools and Middle schools typically have auditoriums ideal for worship services.
- Children's space (lots of classrooms).
- Minimal start-up costs: the national average is $250,000.
- Rental cost is generally much less than most other commercial options.
- High volunteerism initially because of portable church requirements.

Challenges

- Relationship with school administration.
- Storage space for storing portable church items.
- Limited availability to Sunday mornings only.
- Elementary schools usually have inadequate parking, bathrooms, and lack auditoriums
- Typically shorter term leases.
- Church youth don't like to go to their school for church.
- Schools can have visibility and accessibility issues.
- Volunteer burnout after 2 years due to portable church requirements.

Theaters

Advantages

- Location is usually high in visibility and accessibility.
- Safe and appealing for unchurched prospects.
- Parking is generally very generous.
- Minimal start-up costs: the national average is $250,000.
- Rental cost is generally reasonable.
- Large screens with stadium seating for video projection.
- Satellite services can be accommodated with multiple auditoriums within the theater.
- Beverages allowed in the worship center.
- Children love the theater atmosphere.
- High volunteerism initially because of portable church requirements.

Challenges

- Children's space: Most theaters do not have education space so you would need to be creative, especially with infants and preschoolers. Typically the children's space is in front of the stage inside the theater venue.

- Storage space is non-existent.
- Theater AVL systems are usually inadequate for worship and on-site speaking and need to be supplemented.
- A portable platform stage may be needed.
- Limited electrical capacity.
- Limited timeslots available (typically Sunday morning only and often limited to one service time).
- Volunteer burnout after 2 years due to portable church requirements.

Other Churches

Advantages

- Location typically is conducive to what a new church requires.
- Parking should already be commensurate with the size of the facility.
- Children's space readily available (though it may need to be reconfigured).
- Lease or purchase costs are usually reasonable and in some cases free.

Challenges

- Whatever perceptions the community holds about the church that was or is in the current building may have a negative reflection upon your church.
- Upgrade costs can be very expensive if it needs to be retrofitted. You could be looking at the need to add fire sprinklers, additional HVAC, additional plumbing, ADA compliant access, etc. In addition, if this facility was built prior to current zoning requirements, the parking may need to be addressed.
- If sharing the building with another church, you may have limited use and access to the building.
- A Sunday night only option for church services is not a good option for starting a new congregation.

Commercial

Advantages

- More flexibility with children's space.
- Storage space is typically ample.

- Greater availability of times to meet for services, offices hours, etc., typically 24/7.
- If you plan on being there a while, then you can generally obtain a longer-term lease with better rates to include option periods after the initial lease term.
- In many cases, you may have lots of parking and site lighting.

Challenges

- While retail space locations may have great visibility, warehouse locations may have zero visibility and signage.
- Renovation costs can be extensive depending on the condition of the space and the amount of renovation needed.
- CAM – Common Area Maintenance fees can range from less than a dollar per square foot to several dollars which adds to your rental cost.
- Rental rates will vary depending on the type facility and the location.
- Parking spaces, if shared, could impact how many spaces are allocated to your church, especially during normal retail hours.
- Low ceilings (you need 16-18ft minimum clear height for video projection): Many

retail spaces and commercial "flex" spaces have lower roof/ceiling heights than desirable.

- Signage may be limited, and the landlord may impose restrictions.
- Greater risk due to longer-term lease to justify the investment of build-out costs.

Rules of Thumb for New Locations

Every church is unique, meaning that every facility requirement is also unique. However, there are some time tested and proven rules of thumb that will help your church start the planning process to determine some of the preliminary space requirements to meet your ministry objective.

Minimum worship space requirements:

- Worship: Most churches need about 10 square feet per person in the worship seating area. And a wider room is better than a deeper room.
- Lobby: You need about four square feet per person attending worship, plus space for ancillary areas such as cafés, information hubs, and media centers. It is not uncommon that the entire "commons" area is 50-100% of the size of the worship center.
- Platform: This area varies in size, but in rooms arranged for 1,000 people or less, you may assume two square feet per

person in worship, but no less than a total of 400 square feet.

- Restrooms: Never try to save money by downgrading the ladies restroom. Plan on one fixture per 75 people and about 40 square feet per fixture.

Other spaces associated with worship:

- Video and production area: Plan on at least 80 square feet.
- Green room: Plan on at least 15 feet per occupant, and build a restroom near it.
- Back stage: Plan on 50-75% of the platform itself, with access to the rest of the facility without entering through the worship space.

Education Space:

- For children below pre-school age, you will need about 35-45 square feet per child.
- Determine your max kids to teacher ratio and then plan spaces accordingly.
- When planning grade school spaces, think in terms of 25-30 square feet per child.
- Students: Philosophically you need to determine if they will meet concurrently

with the weekend worship services or at another time. If concurrent, then plan on 15-20 square feet per student.

Gotchas to consider:

Most municipalities base the occupancy of a space by the code allowable seating. If your local authority having jurisdiction has adopted the International Building Code, then this equation is done one of 2 ways:

- Loose/flexible seating (i.e. chairs): The calculation for the use of movable chairs is 1 person per 7 square feet in the worship space. So, if you have a room that is 4,200 square feet, the code says that you can fit 600 people in that space (4,200 SF / 7 = 600). However, in reality, you will only be able to fit 400-450 comfortably. This occupancy number is also what is used to determine your ingress/egress doors, toilet fixture count, parking space requirements and heating/cooling loads.
- Fixed seating: Theater seats or other delineated seats that are affixed to the floor. This is calculated on a one-to-one ratio. One seat equals one butt. There are

some real advantages to this kind of seating such as:

- o The occupancy is not unnaturally inflated as with flexible seating.
- o With theater seating, you can actually place the rows closer to each other, allowing you to add one more row for every 9-10 rows and increasing the occupancy.
- o Limits your code minimum parking requirements.
- o Reduces code requirements on HVAC factors and sizing of systems.

Multisite Facility Search Guidelines

If your church is considering a multisite solution either to meet space issues on a main campus or to fulfill your vision to reach a larger market, then the following is a list of criteria to consider as you navigate your options:

- A strategic location within 10-20 minutes driving time from sending campus with strong core base potential. Driving distance in rural communities tends to be 20-30 minutes driving time.
- Worship seating for 400-600 people.
- 20,000 square foot building minimum.
- 18 ft. minimum height ceilings (or to the bottom of the structure if exposed), 22 foot ceiling height ideal.
- Classroom space for children and student ministries.
- 4-6 children classrooms, with combined capacity for 50-60 kids.
- 40-60 square feet per person for total facility (adult, children, administration).
- Large welcoming/gathering/lobby area.

- While "code" may only require 125 spaces (4 to 1 ratio), that is not practical for most churches. Ideally churches need a 1.5 ratio of seats to parking spaces. A 600 seat auditorium would require 400 parking spaces (600 seats / 1.5 spaces = 400 parking spaces).

- Easily visible and accessible from major roads and highways.

- Close to other services (public transportation, parks, restaurants coffee shops, etc.).

- Zoning that allows use by a church.

- A financial investment that doesn't exceed the value of the minimal time you will be there.

- Potential for a long-term, multi-year lease arrangement.

- Get reasonable return on investment. It is ideal to have at least a 3-5 year term option with the ability to renew at your request.

School Rental Guidelines

Schools are one of the most used venues for multisite launches and church planters. They are usually in the heart of your target community and have ample space. Schools are a great place to start a church or multisite campus because of the minimum start-up costs, low rent, and space ideally designed for church use. Schools are the low risk, low cost option in starting a church or launching a multisite campus.

Kevin Jones with Portable Church Industries has worked with hundreds of churches in school facilities. He points out that "rented facilities are a great option solely for finding early on the response to this new congregation. It helps avoid building too large or too small. The flexibility and scalability offers you a great amount of time to learn your new area, show your value in the city, and negotiate a purchase when you go permanent."

As we looked at earlier, there are some negatives. Schools are usually not a good long-term strategy beyond a couple of years because of volunteer burnout and a lack of accessibility 24-7.

Make sure you understand the implications of using a school as your worship facility. In most cases, when a church rents a school, the school district benefits from the rental income, and the school and their staff are left with the headache of hosting a church. This puts you at a disadvantage from the beginning. Here are a few guidelines for school rentals:

1. Communicate to the principal or superintendent the desire to be a partner with the school. Cultivate the relationship.
2. Set aside additional money to be spent on the school for "extras" that can benefit the school and also serve the church. Look for ways to serve and be a blessing to the school.
3. The janitor/custodian is your best friend. Take good care of him or her. The maintenance crew can make or break a relationship. Make sure the janitor has a go-to person in the church to solve weekly problems.
4. Take photos of each classroom before you set up and then return everything exactly back to the original status.

5. Put as little as possible but all that is necessary in the contract. Usually from a renter's viewpoint, less is better in a contract, meaning the less specific, the better.

6. Keep major capital improvements out of the contract if possible unless you can extend the term of the contract. Make those improvements contingent on an extended term, or be applied to the monthly rent.

7. Ask for a 5:30 AM or 6:00 AM access for your tech teams and children set-up, at least initially. In a perfect world, you would get access the night before.

8. Make sure your financial investments don't exceed the value of the minimal time you will be there.

9. Know the school calendar and be proactive. Know when the school play is and when the auditorium may have sets for the school play that need to be in place for a few weeks. It is best if you can be proactive and approach the school about these potential dates before they become an issue.

10. Remember, it is not your building. You are a guest in it. Be a kind guest.

DIY Assessments, Tools, and Evaluations

The following is a list accompanying resources for you and your church to use as you begin the evaluation of various facility and space options.

While we believe that consultation with professionals is critical to a successful evaluation of buildings and facility options, these tools can be a guide as you start this process

All of the below are free...so download away:

Potential Church Facility Assessment

Whether you are considering new property, an existing building or a retail/commercial lease, this assessment will provide you with a grading system to perform a side-by-side evaluation of each to provide you with an analytical approach to your selection process. This multiple tab document can server virtually any facility consideration.

http://coolsolutionsgroup.com/resources?did=26

Facility Option Comparison Matrix

This assessment tool will help your church evaluate the potential costs associate with various types of facilities.

For example, if you are considering renting a school vs. a commercial building vs. buying land, then this tool is for you.

http://coolsolutionsgroup.com/resources?did=27

Non-Building Project Costs

A church development project, whether new construction, renovation, or tenant improvement, includes far more than just the sticks and bricks. This tool will give you a comprehensive list of items that need to be considered when planning your project.

http://coolsolutionsgroup.com/resources?did=28

Worship Space Calculator

Ever wonder how much space you need to accommodate your desired seating? This simple calculator is a simple way to get a preliminary snap shot of the amount of space that may be required.

http://coolsolutionsgroup.com/resources?did=29

Church Plant Timeline

Are you starting a new church? Do you know where to start the process and all the steps that need to be taken? Well, we have the answer. This info-graphic, developed by Christianity Today, provides a visual guide and interactive links to make this journey more manageable to navigate.

http://coolsolutionsgroup.com/resources?did=30

© Copyright 2013 Christianity Today and www.ChurchLawAndTax.com

Made in the USA
San Bernardino, CA
17 October 2014